KEEP YOUR
FEET MOVING

For More Products by TShane Johnson
scan the code above with any phone camera .
Mention "Keep Your Feet Moving" and
receive 50% off the 6 sessions One on One
Coaching with TShane.

TABLE OF CONTENTS

INTRODUCTION

What makes a great leader? What daily actions can you take to grow personally and professionally?

I will cover 7 Principles that will help you so that no matter how bad it sucks, you will always keep your feet moving.

There are specific principles you can follow that will allow you to keep your feet moving with peace, strength, and courage.

- **Principle #1:** I will cover the one thing you can do every day that builds confidence and immediate success.

● **Principle #2:** Moving through your day, you'll face opportunities to put your core values into action when you make decisions. In this section, we'll cover how to *choose* your values.

● **Principle #3:** You'll discover how to exercise your creative muscle, so you'll be able to think and lead in new ways.

● **Principle #4:** Working with a team can be challenging. It is important to remain mindful, authentic, and trusting of others in order to create a cohesive team. We'll cover how to do that in this section.

● **Principle #5:** In order to build a team that gels well, you need trust. We'll discuss four ways you can build trust as a leader.

● **Principle #6:** We'll look at the important concepts of authenticity, self-compassion, and communication.

● **Principle #7:** Strong leadership needs strong mental and physical toughness. I will cover some ways to exercise your mind and body.

These habits are a great way to move one step forward on your journey as a leader.

Now let's look at these daily habits in greater detail.

MAKE YOUR BED

Start your day by making your rack. You won't regret it. When I was in the Marine Corps, 4:30 a.m. reveille that came every single day made this the first thing to accomplish in the morning.

There's even an entire book about it called *Make Your Bed: Little Things That Can Change Your Life ... And Maybe the World* by William H. McRaven. McRaven outlines the benefits of starting each day with a made bed. Most importantly, **it leads to a better day.**

Making the bed is a small thing that goes a long way. This single act is the catalyst for a day of success. Starting the day with positive action leads to more positive action, and before you know it, the stream of inspiration continues to more success.

Being a leader starts with your own source of confidence.

In order to better focus on your own feelings of strength, there are simple behavior modifications you can make that will increase confidence. Part of this is building on success. You can do one small thing – make your bed – and use that as a springboard to more positivity.

STICKING TO A ROUTINE

Start the day off right with a definite action that marks the beginning of your day. Making your bed is a great way to cue your mind to kick into gear and start the day. By doing this, you establish a solid morning routine.

Making your bed can strengthen your ability to lead. Here's how:

1. **Consistent structure.** Routines are an important part of each day because they

KEEP YOUR FEET MOVING

provide a consistent structure.

> ○ **This structure provides stability that is key to outstanding leadership** because it gives you strength and peace of mind at the very beginning of the day.

2. **Predictability.** By knowing precisely what your morning looks like, you are able to avoid any unnecessary confusion or indecision.

> ○ This predictability decreases anxiety because your mind doesn't need to be riddled with unnecessary forecasts about what your day will be like.

3. **Greater self-discipline.** Sticking to a morning routine increases self-discipline in all areas. This habit requires intention and patience. This ritual will provide an inner strength that will permeate all of your affairs, making you a stronger

leader.

4. **Satisfaction.** Regardless of the day you've had, you always get to come home to a made bed. That is where the satisfaction of a morning routine comes full circle. When you unmake your bed and tuck yourself in at night, you'll feel a sense of achievement regardless of outside stressors.

It's important to set up the first hour or two of your day to be the same every morning. Start with making your bed.

See if you can go the first hour of your day without checking your email or social media. **Remain peaceful and slowly begin your day.** This will feel much more satisfying than the shock of the alarm clock jolting you into reality.

If you have trouble sleeping, establishing a nightly routine is a great way to get your sleep in order.

Turn off technology at least one hour before bed. Take time to slow your mind and relax. It can be hard to go from work-mode to chill-mode, but **this transition is essential.** If you don't take time to let yourself slow your thoughts and be mindful, you'll likely experience more stress.

If you can always count on your mornings and your nights looking the same, you'll feel a better sense of security throughout your day.

Life is always uncertain, and that's one of the only things you can be sure of. However, you can implement a structure that will help tether you to the present moment.

Regardless of how much your mind wanders throughout the day, regardless of the ups and downs, you'll always have a fresh setting in which to start and end your day. This contributes to a more peaceful environment at home.

When you feel refreshed and energized, you're more likely to approach your interactions with the same attitude.

Being a leader requires a quiet stability. One way to work towards that consistency and dependability is by making your bed in the morning.

ACT ACCORDING TO YOUR MORAL VALUES

CHOOSING YOUR VALUES

Values are core concepts that can be used as guideposts for living. There are limitless possibilities for what values you can use to guide your leadership. Based on how you live and work, you can evaluate your priorities and decide upon your core values.

These techniques can help you clarify your values:

1. **What type of leader do you want to be?** An effective way to approach the prospect of choosing your values is by looking at what kind of leader you want to be. How do you want to treat difficult situations?

14

When have you felt like a good leader in the past?

2. **Write down the things that are important to you.** While choosing your values, it may be helpful to write them down and think through what it will look like when you are acting upon those values.

3. **Prioritize.** It's better to choose a small selection of values rather than dozens. At first, you can choose any values that sound applicable. Once you have a good selection, narrow down those values based on how important they are to your mission.

Sticking to just a few guiding principles makes the evaluation of decisions much simpler.

HOW CAN YOU MAKE DECISIONS BASED ON VALUES?

Your values represent what you really stand for. **When you're acting according to your values, you're turning them into verbs and living them out loud.**

For example, if you value honesty, you may act according to that value by remaining honest in all of your interactions. If you value reliability, you may demonstrate that value by being consistently available to those who rely on you.

Having a set of core values can be a sort of safety net in situations that may be uncomfortable or unclear. By looking at these values, you can make a decision based on the type of leader you want to be.

Envision what your life might be like if you based your decisions and actions on the principles you most value. When you see yourself in that light, you'll be motivated to move towards that positive action in your own daily life.

When you're leading a team, it can be hard to see what the future holds. **Just because you're lighting the way doesn't mean you always know where you're going.**

Use values like street lamps lighting the way. You may make a wrong move or find that you've made a bit of a detour, but when you reassess the situation and align your values, you'll be better able to do the next right thing.

BE CREATIVE

Creativity is a major factor in leadership. In fact, it frequently separates the good from the great. Outstanding leaders are creative.

An ability to think quickly (and to do so outside the box) is a skill that you can harness by embracing creativity in new ways. Try these endeavors to spark your creativity.

WRITE

Practice these writing techniques:

1. **Journaling.** There are many excellent benefits of keeping a journal:

   ○ Consistently journaling can help heal you emotionally.

Reliability Dependability
Integrity, Respect, Persevere...
Innovation
vision + Discovery
Ability Flexibility
Ingenuity

○ A journal is an excellent resource during times of stress or confusion.

○ By getting your thoughts out of your head and onto a piece of paper, you may be able to stand back and see your concerns from a new perspective.

2. **Morning Pages.** One writing practice that you can implement today is an activity called "morning pages" presented by Julia Cameron in her book *The Artist's Way.* **Morning Pages are three pages of stream-of-consciousness writing that are best done as a part of your morning routine**.

○ Writing like this gives you an immediate outlet where you can lay out any thoughts that may be bogging you down.

○ Think of your Morning Pages time as an opportunity to clean out your mind and rid yourself of unnecessary anxieties or cares. Leave all of your concerns on the page so that you can go out and embrace your day.

○ Do three pages seem like too many? **You don't even need to complete a whole page.** Avoid pressuring yourself to complete three pages. Over time, you can work your way up.

MAKE SOMETHING

Whether your specialty is programming or tap dancing, making something opens your mind to being creative in new ways. New experiences in creating art unleash your mind because you get to stretch it in new directions.

It can be intimidating to paint a painting or make a coffee mug from clay. There's no need to do something that sparks immense anxiety. However, you *can* challenge yourself a little bit.

See what it's like to make something new:

1. **Start simply.** Begin by choosing a coloring book and your favorite color markers. You can work your way up from there. Eventually, you might try painting or sculpture!

    ○ **The important thing is to choose something that is a different type of creativity than you're used to.**

2. **Reap the benefits:**

    ○ Trying new creative endeavors leads to decreased anxiety and increased peace-of-mind.

○ Being creative means taking risks. It means believing in the impossible and dreaming the biggest dreams. By embracing new ways of thinking, your mind will awaken to new pathways of innovation.

○ Being creative also allows for faster and more effective problem solving, a critical skill for strong leaders.

This new type of experience will ripple into many aspects of your leadership style, enabling you to think in new ways.

BE FLEXIBLE

Part of creativity is the ability to be flexible, especially when challenges appear in your path.

Obstacles don't mean that the path is ruined. Instead, obstacles tell us that there's a more effective route to our goal. Sometimes, they lead us to the goal in a way we would never have seen without that hiccup.

Try these strategies to strengthen your ability to be flexible:

1. **Go with the flow.** Because life is uncertain and (unfortunately) we can't control everything, it's especially important to remain flexible during times of stress or confusion. With constant upgrades in technology and efficiency, the way the team operates is continuously evolving.

2. **Keep an open mind.** Flexibility requires an ability to meet unusual circumstances with an open mind and motivation to push forward. **Outstanding leaders respond to the needs of their team and take steps accordingly.**

○ For example, when a potential issue appears, it may be necessary to set aside the planned work for the day to address this need.

○ Responding to this deviation can be handled calmly and seamlessly. Instead of resisting the current needs, embrace the new direction, and see where it leads.

○ This tactic will also ensure that the highest priority items are done first, even if they sneak up. Teams run like a well-oiled machine when everyone is willing to have an open mind.

3. **Let go of expectations.** As a leader, it's essential to be able to let go of certain expectations. This can be difficult to do, but it will help foster new ideas and attention to detail.

○ One behavior modification you can do today is to *imagine* what it would be like to let go of expectations. You don't even have to let go of the expectations yet. Simply *imagine what it might be like* to enter the day without them.

○ Let go of your idea of how the day must go. **What would happen if you let go completely and addressed the present moment?**

○ Instead of thinking five steps ahead of your current conversation, try focusing on each word and each idea as they come.

○ **The ability to stay present in the moment is essential to remaining flexible.**

○ By sticking to what you know now, you can choose your next step wisely.

Resisting the present moment is the fast lane to frustration. By letting go of your expectations, you can embrace the flexibility you need to lead others forward. You're able to accept and address each moment as it comes.

PRACTICE MINDFULNESS

Mindfulness has become hugely popular, and for good reason! There are many benefits to mindfulness that bring about noticeable change. The benefits of a regular and consistent mindfulness practice are overwhelming. Especially in moments of stress, this emotion-regulation tool brings about peace in the storm.

As a leader, it's especially important to be able to stay calm and lead your team out of a crisis. The inner peace that mindfulness brings you is ideal in helping you through such situations.

By practicing mindfulness for just 10 minutes a day, you'll enjoy the benefits that come with a consistent routine.

There are a number of easy ways to dive into a mindfulness practice.

MINDFULNESS MEDITATION

Mindfulness meditation is a powerful way to embrace the miracle of mindfulness. Jon Kabat-Zinn (an expert in mindfulness) defines it as "paying attention in a particular way: on purpose, in the present moment, and non-judgmentally."

The purpose of mindfulness meditation is to come to the present moment with awareness. There is no goal. The goal isn't even to have *no* thoughts. It's nearly impossible to have no thoughts. So, don't worry when your mind wanders.

Discover how mindfulness meditation is as simple as breathing:

1. **Get ready to meditate.** Find a quiet spot where you can sit comfortably on the floor or in a chair. Sit upright but remain comfortable. You can keep your eyes open

and focus on one spot in front of you, or you can shut your eyes.

2. **Focus on your breathing.** Feel yourself inhaling. You can even think to yourself, "Oh, here I am, inhaling." Exhale. Notice, "Oh, now I am exhaling." Try to do this consistently.

3. **Notice when your mind wanders.** Your mind will naturally wander. The moment that you notice your mind wandering is the truest moment of awareness.

4. **Bring your focus back to your breathing.** You can gently return your focus to your breath. You haven't failed at meditating. In fact, you've succeeded!

Mindfulness meditation strengthens focus – a change that occurs after just a couple of weeks of consistent meditation.

If you tend to be an anxious person, meditation is the right thing for you. It may seem daunting to sit quietly for more than a few minutes, but you can work your way up to a time that you're comfortable with. If you can stick through a sometimes-uncomfortable beginning, a steady meditation practice will decrease anxiety the more you do it.

MINDFULNESS PRACTICES

Depending on your style and preferred coping skills, you can develop a mindfulness practice that consists of engaging in activities that work for you.

By setting aside dedicated time to practice mindfulness each day (start with 5 minutes!), a residual calmness will wash over the rest of your day.

Try these mindfulness practices:

1. **Sort buttons.** One fun mindfulness practice requires one big jar and a lot of

buttons. Dump out all of the buttons and then organize them into whatever categories you want. Arrange them by size, shape, color, in order from smallest to largest, or anything you want.

○ **The point is to get lost in the moment and focus on what is right in front of you.** Instead of leaving your current moment and jumping back in time or far into the future, try seeing what it feels like to really be here right now.

○ Arranging buttons may not seem like much, but you might find that it's the break you need.

2. **Pursue creative activities.** When you embrace your creativity and pursue creative endeavors, you can practice mindfulness.

○ Try coloring in a coloring book for 10 minutes.

○ You can paint a painting with your favorite colors and pay careful attention to each brush stroke. Be intentional with each color. Feel what it's like to hold a paintbrush in your hand.

3. **Get back to nature.** Perhaps you need a break to go breathe fresh air in nature. Whether you take your dog to the dog park, head to the beach, or go for a hike, immersing yourself in nature is a great way to practice mindfulness.

○ There is something very healing about being outside and feeling free.

○ Spend time each week in nature, observing the wonders of life going on around you.

MINDFULNESS IN YOUR DAILY LIFE

If you don't want to carve out a specific time to do a mindfulness activity, you can find ways to seamlessly integrate mindfulness into your existing daily routines.

Try these strategies:

1. **Start by brushing your teeth.** While you brush your teeth, try focusing on the bristles on your gums, or the taste of the minty toothpaste on your toothbrush. Maybe you can smell the minty freshness filling your mouth. Perhaps you hear the bristles brushing in small circles, just like your dentist always reminds you.

2. **Take your dog for a walk.** While you walk, focus on details of the landscape right in front of you. Try not to bother yourself with the typical commentary that occurs throughout the day. As you walk,

observe.

- ○ Observe the colors of the leaves, the sounds of the cars, and the barking from other dogs as you walk past them. You can focus on your heels hitting the ground, and then your toes.

- ○ **Simply take in, with all of your senses, what is occurring in the present moment.**

- ○ When your mind wanders, take notice, and return your attention to what is going on in the present moment.

3. **Eat mindfully.** Eating is a great way to practice mindfulness. So frequently, we find ourselves rushing through our meal, talking with others, or even doing work while eating. Rarely do we truly pay attention to each bite we take and each

taste we taste.

○ Pay close attention to your food.
Take in the smell and texture of
every bite.

Outstanding leaders practice mindfulness.
And their team members receive the benefits of
this practice.

By practicing mindfulness, you'll be able to
retain an open mind and a clear head. When
facing obstacles, you won't be met with stress.
Instead, a consistent calm will remain in the
moment, and it will be easy to focus on the task
at hand.

Because mindfulness so improves attention, you
may begin noticing things you've never seen
before. Attention to detail is a skill best
developed through mindfulness.

You'll also notice greater feelings of fulfillment
and fewer feelings of pressure or stress. **Your**

ability to regulate emotion, manage stress, and stay calm will radiate from you.

This sort of energy is contagious, and soon, your whole team will also feel at ease. Mindfulness will enable you to create a culture of calm. By doing so, you're creating a team of people who are secure and willing. This can lead to powerful new ideas that will continue to make the world a better place.

TRUST OTHERS

Sometimes, being a leader means taking a step back. While taking on a new challenge, it can be best to give your team members the opportunity to embrace new growth.

Follow these strategies to empower your team and lead them to greater success.

DELEGATE

Instead of taking the lead as you usually do, let another hard worker take a stab at it. Delegating allows you to get work done through the efforts of collaborative teamwork.

Your leadership will shine brightest through the accomplishments of others. Watch the magic that can happen when you give your team the power to venture to their own success.

Delegation fosters a culture of trust throughout the community. When you demonstrate trust in others, they will trust you in return. The appreciation of respect and trust will lead to positive steps forward and new developments.

Trust is one of the keys to developing a well-functioning and dedicated team. When team members appreciate and help one another, more work will get done because there is less fear associated with work pressures.

EMPOWER YOUR TEAM

Allowing others to take the reins can at first seem counterintuitive. If you already know how to do something well, it can be challenging to let someone who doesn't know how to do it make an attempt.

However, this practice is important. By allowing others to take new leaps, they will feel more secure in pursuing the team's mission.

Finding creative ways to empower a team can be difficult. The most important thing to do is acknowledge hard work. You don't need to provide positive praise every day, or even every week. But it's important to voice appreciation for those who go above and beyond.

ALLOW ROOM FOR INNOVATION

A culture of trust and follow-through will develop leaders within the community. These leaders will inspire their peers. Such spread-out leadership results in a special kind of collaboration. When all parties feel present, valued, and empowered, innovation can take place.

See how this transformation happens:

1. **Get started.** At first, new ideas and taking risks can seem intimidating or daunting. It's easier to stick to the tried and true ways of doing things. But what if there's something better? What if there's something right under your nose that

39

could change the world?

2. **The best way to brilliance is with a team of dedicated people:**

   ○ In an environment that feels safe and non-judgmental, people are more likely to communicate while collaborating with each other. Peers will create small think-tanks, where no one is afraid of a bad idea. The very best ideas frequently evolve from an original not-so-awesome idea.

   ○ Collaboration ensures movement towards big, creative goals. With greater connectivity, resources for growth are plentiful.

3. **Think long term.** With each passing year, there is even more inspiring innovation. That innovation was born out of brave leaders taking leaps. The future is happening at every moment. There is

constant newness. Constant freshness. Always forward.

Allowing everyone on your team to be a leader and giving everyone the power to pursue growth inevitably leads to innovation. As their leader, you've inspired those around you to create this environment of success.

GIVE DIRECTION

Have no fear, letting others take new risks doesn't mean that you have to stand by while mistakes are made. These situations are great opportunities for you to provide guidance and mentorship.

You can always teach something new to those you lead. As a leader, you have the opportunity to guide those who have never walked the path that you have.

Combining the wisdom of experience and the clarity of newness gives a fresh perspective on the big picture.

41

You will also benefit by allowing yourself to be flexible and open-minded while learning from those you lead.

BE AUTHENTIC

In her book *The Gifts of Imperfection: Let Go of Who You're Supposed to Be and Embrace Who You Are,* Brene Brown defines authenticity as:

> "A collection of choices that we have to make every day. It's about the choice to show up and be real. The choice to be honest. The choice to let our true selves be seen."

This definition allows values to take the lead.

See how living according to your values, supports being authentic:

1. **Your values can remind you to be authentic.** If your values are based on the person you truly are (or the person you're growing into), allowing them to guide you is a great way to remind yourself to stay

authentic.

○ When you stray from your values
(as we all do from time to time, or
from minute to minute), you can
check-in with yourself to evaluate
whether you're truly being
authentic.

○ For example, after you've left an
interaction, you can ask yourself –
"Did I stand strong? Did I show up
at the present moment?"

○ When the answer to these
questions is no, you don't need to
be hard on yourself. It's sometimes
difficult to be authentic. In times of
anxiety or stress, it's easy to fall
into people-pleasing behaviors.
Sometimes the ego takes over,
especially in positions of
leadership.

○ Remember to be self-compassionate when you find that you were actually worried more about looking good than you were about being authentic.

2. **Being authentic doesn't mean you need to share your deepest personal details with everyone you meet.**

○ Every interaction you have may have a different tone – casual, familial, professional, even cold – each of these calls for authenticity in a slightly different way.

○ You can be authentic in a setting that is appropriate professionally. **Remain authentic at work by allowing your core values to guide you.** Perhaps, in a work setting, your vocabulary or tone of voice changes. That's okay. You're being authentic as long as *you* are shining through.

Leaders who remain true to their authentic selves are likely to be well-respected and well-liked.

By owning your true self and acting according to your values, other wonderful things will happen. A feeling of ease will permeate through the workspace. Since there isn't a secret persona you're trying to pull off, you don't need to pretend to be something you're not.

Authenticity means accepting exactly who you are and showing up to each present moment.

Practicing authenticity requires self-compassion. Being self-compassionate is another challenging task that seems obvious, but doesn't always come naturally.

SELF-COMPASSION

Self-compassion is pivotal to authenticity because it allows us to be okay with being ourselves.

Plus, part of being a truly outstanding leader is having compassion - for others and for yourself. By changing your negative self-talk and addressing your downfalls with compassion instead of self-criticism, you'll notice an obvious shift towards positivity.

Self-compassion builds resilience, it increases productivity, and it decreases negative rumination.

Dr. Kristin Neff, a researcher who has taken on the study of self-compassion, explains: "Instead of mercilessly judging and criticizing yourself for various inadequacies or shortcomings, self-compassion means you are kind and understanding when confronted with personal failings."

In her book, *Self-Compassion,* Dr. Neff outlines three elements of self-compassion:

- Self-kindness
- Common humanity
- Mindfulness

Let's look closer at these qualities of self-compassion:

1. **Self-kindness.** When you make a mistake on your leadership journey, be grateful for an opportunity to practice self-compassion by changing your self-talk.

    ○ Changing your self-talk is a process. It begins by observing when you're being critical. And then you replace those critical thoughts with self-loving thoughts. Eventually, this process will become automatic.

○ Follow these steps:

i. **Be aware.** Notice your self-talk when you're in a negative headspace after making a mistake.

ii. **Observe the negative feeling.** If you find yourself repeating negative phrases to yourself, take a moment to bring your awareness to that line of thinking.

iii. **Change your thought.** Try writing down one of those negative thoughts. Next to it, write down an opposite and true *positive* phrase that you can repeat to yourself instead.

2. **Common humanity.** Feeling negative about ourselves can often be isolating.

3. **A key part of self-compassion is recognizing the common humanity that runs through all of us.**

   ○ When you make a mistake, or something doesn't go as planned, see what it's like to feel a sense of connection with all who have felt the way you do.

   ○ Practicing this over time leads to more compassion for others. When your teammates make a mistake or take the wrong route, you'll be more forgiving and less blaming.

4. **Mindfulness.** Mindfulness is another major factor in self-compassion. When you approach a situation with mindfulness, you'll find that you won't feel so wrapped up in the situation.

   ○ You can use mindfulness when you're having a whirlwind of negative self-talk. **Instead of**

letting your thoughts sweep you away into a black hole of self-doubt, try coming into a mindful awareness of yourself.

○ This will help you put things into perspective and take a step back.

SELF-COMPASSION EXERCISES

There are simple exercises that you can do to make self-compassion a part of your usual thought processes. You can set aside time, or you can integrate self-compassion into your daily life.

Try these techniques to increase your self-compassion:

1. **Go out to eat.** Take yourself out for your favorite food and keep the thought in your mind that you're doing it because you love yourself. During your meal, repeat self-loving phrases. Try to go

51

through the whole meal just saying nice things to yourself.

○ If you have a hard time coming up with nice things to say about yourself on the spot, try writing yourself a short note or letter stating objective facts, such as "I have potential. I am capable. I am a hard worker."

○ You can also refer to this note during times of stress or feelings of failure.

2. **Meditate.** Starting a meditation practice, as we've already learned, has many benefits. One of them is an increase in self-compassion.

○ During your meditation practice, try repeating a positive mantra to yourself. It should be simple, believable, and easy to remember. You can bring this mantra with you and think of it throughout the day.

3. **Remind yourself how great you are.** A great way to remember to pause for self-compassion is by setting reminders on your phone to go off a few times a day. When you hear your phone ding, you can use that small interruption to say some kind phrases to yourself.

You're not the only one who will feel better as a result of self-compassion. Those you lead will reap the benefits as well. You may even notice that your ability to be kind to yourself inspires others to do the same.

It's a common misconception that beating ourselves up leads to fewer mistakes in the future. Unfortunately, there will always be mistakes in the future. Always. That's part of life. This is where having a self-compassion practice comes in handy.

By starting a self-compassion practice now, you'll handle future hurdles with ease.

Self-compassion also gives us the ability to communicate authentically. We may say something we regret or suggest a bad idea. Self-compassion allows us to move on from that moment and go to the next. It provides the courage needed to take risks and communicate.

COMMUNICATE

Authenticity requires clear communication. While it's a good thing that others cannot read minds, it can be frustrating when you want them to understand your vision exactly. In order to get your message across, you'll need to develop ways to help others understand your goals.

Better yet, let them be a part of the goal-making process. Get insight from others and give direct, thoughtful feedback on their ideas.

Include these ideas in your daily interactions to strengthen your ability to communicate clearly:

1. **Listen.** A huge part of communication is listening. By listening to others and observing their actions, you're able to gain knowledge of what they do or do not understand.

   ○ **Others can tell when you're not listening to them.** They'll act accordingly, and that's how miscommunication begins.

   ○ It's a good practice to only have one conversation at a time. This allows all parties to feel like they're getting the attention they deserve so they can have their voice heard.

   ○ While others are talking, taking brief notes will help you comprehend and remember the information.

2. **Pay attention to your body language.** Body Language plays a significant role in communication. In fact, **over half of our communication is nonverbal.** When you're communicating, ensure your body language is delivering your ideas accurately.

   ○ Keep an open and upright posture and make eye contact.

3. **Understand what you may need to communicate.** Before you pass along a plan, project, or idea, work on clarifying it for yourself before giving it to others. It might be helpful to write down key points, words, or goals so you can have guideposts while communicating.

Communication is essential to progress. In order to move forward effectively and authentically, communication is key. When you say something, let your actions communicate your ideas as well. Take a moment to come back to your breath, assess your values, and take on a fresh perspective.

Authenticity isn't easy. Outstanding leaders have the courage to be fearlessly authentic in all areas of their lives. It takes practice, self-compassion, patience, and willingness. However, the payoff is worth every moment of uncomfortable learning.

EXERCISE

Healthy leaders are happy leaders. And happy leaders are effective and productive. A great way to achieve a positive state of mind and body is through exercise.

Regular exercise does more than boost your metabolism and muscle strength. It also lifts your mood and gives you energy.

MENTAL HEALTH

Exercise is one of the most effective ways to amplify positive mental states. Besides lifting your mood, exercise also helps with depression, anxiety, and ADHD.

By exercising, you are increasing blood flow to the brain. This increase in blood flow leads to the production of chemicals that make you happy. For example, serotonin is released when you engage in physical exercise. The production of serotonin is related to depression because when people are depressed, less serotonin is produced.

There are a number of workouts that especially increase mood, such as Yoga.

Here's how Yoga can help:

- By taking an hour to go to a Yoga class, you're giving yourself the gift of mindfulness. Yoga is a great mindfulness and exercise activity because you're focused solely on your body and what it can do.

- Listening to or watching the instructor and then following the movements requires immense focus. You may notice that during Yoga class, you lose track of time or forget to think. This is because you're fully in the present moment, not bogged down by outside distractions.

- With Yoga, you don't need to put too much pressure on yourself to be more flexible than you are. **You can practice accepting yourself just the way you are, knowing that you're always growing.**

- Yoga takes patience, and the best place to practice that patience is with yourself.

- Take an opportunity to be self-compassionate and think about all of the amazing things your body is capable of. It's okay to sit down and take a break on your mat during yoga class. If there's a move you can't do, you can simply give yourself permission to take it easy and only do as much as you can do.

Cardiovascular routines such as running, hiking, boxing, and dancing also have excellent mood-boosting benefits that you'll feel during the workout, after the workout, and consistently with regular practice.

You can start by getting your body moving for 30 minutes a day just a few times a week.

There's no need to run a marathon the first time you put on running shoes. Go easy on yourself. It won't take long into your workout for you to notice that you're feeling clear headed. Endorphins are being released in your brain. This collection of brain chemicals directly increases your energy level and mood.

PHYSICAL HEALTH

When you first start exercising, it works well to **set small goals for yourself and your exercise routine.** Start with a 30-minute outdoor walk with your dog. Work your way up to longer work out sessions.

Move toward just one goal at a time, building upon success after success.

Joining a gym is a great way to get some accountability for your goals. You can get to know a community of healthy people and use the gym resources to learn about new workouts and how to be healthier.

Does the idea of joining a gym make you feel uncomfortable?

These tips can help:

- It can be intimidating to join a gym or even enter the doors. Don't worry; you don't need to wait until you're in shape to feel comfortable working out.

- One way to start getting comfortable with the gym is by going in and asking for a tour when you get your membership. Ask questions and be observant. This is a great way to get to know a staff member, and it will help you feel more comfortable asking questions in the future.

- Once you have your gym membership, the next step is going to the gym. **Start by**

telling yourself that all you have to do is walk on the treadmill for 10 minutes. No one is timing your workout, so you don't need to feel shame about how long you're in the gym.

- If all you do is walk on the treadmill for 10 minutes, you've had a successful workout. You've conquered the fear that so many have when going to the gym. Remember, these feelings of insecurity are a great way to connect to common humanity.

- **You can rest assured knowing that nearly everyone in the gym is or has been just as intimidated as you are.** Use this as a way to connect to those around you.

Feel inspired to take better care of your body! Enjoy the mental and physical benefits that exercise can bring you. Step up to a higher plane in your leadership abilities.

CONCLUSION

There will be missteps. There will be difficult days. **A truly outstanding leader uses coping skills and simple behavior modifications to come back into focus and keep pushing towards the impossible.** Being a leader is a big responsibility, and there is no single right way to do it.

Start your day with a positive action and let that singular action ripple through the rest of the day. Having a routine will anchor your day in a way that feels whole. An act as small as making your bed can set the tone for your behavior in each interaction you have and each decision that you make.

It feels good to do good.

Decide what "good" means to you by evaluating your values and connecting them to concrete actions you can take. Come up with a set of a few core values that you can use as a compass in the forest of leadership. Living according to values provides a clarity of mind that is difficult to come by.

Embrace creativity and new ways of thinking.

You can do this by implementing simple practices such as coloring in a coloring book or taking a painting class. It may not seem immediately connected, but **creatively stretching your mind will lead to more creative leadership.**

Being creative will also keep you flexible and able to think quickly in unexpected situations. You may think that you're supposed to go one way, but when you stick too closely to these expectations, you may miss a better route. Creative activities will broaden your horizons and train your mind to think in new ways.

Practice mindfulness.

Outstanding leaders have a unique ability to be mindful. Practicing mindfulness is essential to the core of what it means to be a leader. Making behavior modifications as simple as noticing when you're brushing your teeth leads to more peace of mind.

Trust others.

Consistent stability makes those you lead feel comfortable and trusting. You may also find that you trust others in new ways when you feel more secure in the present moment.

Trusting others is essential to leadership. While you're leading a team, you're not the only one making the engine run. **Teamwork is required to attain success.** In order to be a great leader, you must delegate and allow those you lead to take new risks and try new opportunities.

This idea can be hard to put into practice because it requires a new level of letting go - a new level of accepting that you cannot control everything. Allowing others to try new things is a great way for you to display your leadership abilities by being a great teacher.

The best way to lead is by being true to who you are.

You cannot lead if you're trying to be something you're not at the same time. That's too distracting. It will waste your time.

You'll garner more respect from your team members if you give yourself permission to show each moment precisely who you are.

Communicate clearly.

You can help others understand and see what you see by practicing clear and concise communication. Whether you're asking for help or giving direction, communication can make or break a team.

Exercise.

Exercising will uplift your mood, clarify your thinking, bring you energy, and support vigorous health. It will also help you develop strength and discipline. Maintain your health and build qualities essential for leadership with exercise!

Embrace your leadership.

It can be a daunting task to embrace leadership. The right answer is not always clear, and many people are counting on you for direction. By implementing simple habits in your daily life, **you can shine like the true leader you are.**

In practicing these routines, you'll be better equipped to lead in new directions. You'll be able to explore new territory and take on new opportunities.

The best way to start is by starting. Start anywhere. Choose one thing and start with that. And then go, move forward. Lead.

Made in the USA
Columbia, SC
26 January 2023

10241700R00043